Along The Way

Reflections and Recollections

of

Wayne Gore

Foreword

This book is dedicated to my
siblings, Judy Frankel, Molena Pantenburg,
and Keith Gore. All three have at one
time or another walked into a dark valley and
survived to emerge at the other end.
Special thanks to my wife Ann for her support
And patience.

Index

Page 1   Virginia
Page 3   The New River
Page 5   Across The River
Page 7   I Thought I Could Fly
Page 9   Wildflowers
Page 11 Splendor
Page 13 A Dream
Page 15 Dana
Page 17 This Mystical Place
Page 19 Mysteries
Page 21 If You Should Go
Page 23 The Memory Jar
Page 25 Death
Page 27 The Wicked Witch
Page 29 He Never Danced
Page 31 We Are Falling

* All poems are preceded by a prologue on the even numbered page preceding that particular poem. This is my attempt to express my motivation and insight for that particular poem.

Page 33 Tommy Peacock and the Monkey
Page 39 Bobby Hale and the Cowboy Suit
Page 45 Barneys Wooden Leg
Page 53 Grandmas Crock-pot
Page 59 The Watermelon Truck
Page 65 The Minstrel Show

Virginia

A surly fresco of blinding orange and yellow, colliding with an unimpeachable red adorned the valleys and trails of my youth. My senses peaked to a lighthearted crescendo of autumn colors.
Oh, Virginia of yesteryear surely you can extend your grace once more and shower me with your beauty. Your rivers, streams and mountains second only to Gods own Eden.

Prologue to The New River

For all of you who grew up near a river no explanation is necessary about the strength we derive from such an experience. We hold in our memories the wonderful gifts of nature we derived from these adventures. We are grateful for the bounty of those Memories we hold in reserve.

New River

Mighty river you are my friend
You come and go, then come again.
An eternal journey is your claim to fame,
You answer not to the mortals game.

Teasing your way thru the valleys below
Making your way with an ebb and flow.
White men, black men and Indians alike
Have shared your journey, this wondrous flight.

With all your peace and glorious charm
you warm our hearts and make us one.
Your friend the mountain will protect your path
Ushering you homeward to the sea at last.

A sullen beauty from an ancient age
Bountiful, sleepy and full of grace.
Sea to sky and to the earthly plane
Your journey complete you must start again.

Prologue to Across The River

Never entirely satisfied with our status qou
we continue to look for greener pastures.
Fishing on the banks of the New River was an
exercise in temptation. The other side of the
river was always the most alluring.
I knew if I were only to get to the other side
of the river the fishing would be much better.

Across The River

Across the river a meadow does lie,
green and lush with grass so high.
I see this place and it calls to me,
To come, to play, to come and see.

I struggle the rapids and currents wide
And finally reach the other side.
In my amazement what do I see?
The other side beckoning to me.

Prologue to I thought I could fly

Growing up in an environment of freedom
allows the mind of a small child to
accomplish things they will never attempt
once they become adults.
As we age we lose the ability to dream as
only small children can do. I know I took
many trips beyond my domain as a small boy in
the Virginia mountains. I traveled to
unimaginable places and always returned safely.

I Thought I Could Fly

There was a time I thought I could fly
I don't know how and I don't know why.
I touched the stars in a moonlit sky
Pinching the clouds as I flew by.
That was back then when I thought I could fly.

Lighthearted and wondrous I was in awe
To chase a comet across the sky.
Larks and eagles were my best friends
Along with a hawk and an occasional wren.
When I thought I could fly, that was back then

I flew to Egypt then to Spain, to the great
China wall then home again. I raced along with
Thundering storms, teasing the lightning and riding
The wind. That was when I thought I could fly
But that was way back, way back when.

As all journeys must start all journeys must end
We can all travel about if only within.
I plunged thru the heavens end over end,
Never stopping to ask the why or the when.
That was way back, back when I was Ten.

Prologue to Wildflowers

Death is a sorrowful visitor when you
are a child. It is Uninvited and mysterious,
steadfast and unyielding. I experienced
the loss of my fifteen year old sister when
I was thirteen years old. I remember it daily
although fifty odd years have passed.

Wildflowers

I walked the dusty road today
to visit you with much to say.
Your memory beckons I have found
since last I walked this holy ground.

The day is hot, the sun moves slow.
I glance about where wildflowers grow.
They remind me of you from an earlier day,
here a short time then on your way.

Wildflowers and God's good grace
have drawn me again to this fair place
to share this time, to ease the pain
till time stands still and we meet again.

Our time was short, we did not know
the end was near and you had to go.
So much to say before chill winds blow
but I will return when wildflowers grow.

Prologue to Splendor

It was one of those moments that comes
once in a lifetime. You realize all is right
with the world, and you are lucky enough
to observe it. Beauty surrounds you,
clinging to you for very brief second,
Then you become aware.

Splendor

Splendor arrives an unannounced guest,
in the twinkle of an eye
during the course of a breath.

A flashing smile, a gentle touch-
just a feeling or maybe a nudge.

The beauty and grace of a summer day
A glimpse from God to show the way.

Forget your fame, it was long ago.
Court tomorrow it is where you go.

Grasp the moment, make it last,
remember it always for it shall pass.

Prologue to A Dream

Your first, most serious love, the
one that kept you awake nights as
you tried to make sense of it all, the
first love, the one that robbed you of all
Your senses.

A Dream

I chased you thru a dream last night,
Pursuing you with fancied flight.
Searching in a starry sky.
Aching for a fleeting sight.

I searched all stars and portals beyond
Driven on by a lovers bond.
On past Polaris and the Southern Cross-
I searched until all hope was lost.

Then near dawn at Heaven's gate
I plunged homeward to a lonely fate.
I found you there where I had been,
I'll never search the stars again.

Prologue to Dana

Sitting on a sofa during a quiet time, reading a book or listening to the leaves rustle outside your window. Thinking of a Loved one who has passed on. Suddenly from nowhere you sense someone passing by your shoulder. There only long enough to catch your attention, then gone.

Dana

I saw you there in the shadows,
in the corner of my eye.
You darted past without a sound.
A shadow only I can see.
A shadow soft as a memory and
fleeting as a whisper.
I turned to better glimpse you;
Again I was too slow.

Prologue to This Mystical place

Have we not all spent time wondering
about the eternal workings of the universe
and our place in all of this? Where do we fit
and how does the puzzle come together for us.
I suspect we have the questions
and God has the answers.

This Mystical Place

We traverse this mystical place, not with
Leaps and bounds but slowly with simple faith.
Our fortunes rise and fall as the shifting tides
With no known course that reason abides.

Our paths unsure, we feel our way
As doubting children who are ever astray.
We hook our fortunes to a shooting star
And wonder how we've come so far.

We travel with awe as at Ocean's edge,
On shifting sand or a shaky ledge.
Holding our nerve and trusting our heart,
Making our way as we stop and start.

God waits for us as we search for Him;
We bridge the Abyss and try again.
Longing and searching for another way
We travel alone throughout our days.

We make this journey as a matter of will,
Few answers we find, but we travel still.
Maybe at the close of day
Maybe, just maybe we will find our way.

Prologue to Mysteries

How do you resolve the mysteries
you encounter daily? Do you allow
the mysteries to slip by unchallenged
or do you somewhere deep down ask
yourself about them as they appear?
What about the why and what
About the when.

Mysteries

On a dark night when the stars all glow,
Tell me again -where does the half-moon go

When winter appears with a withering snow,
Tell me again-where does the warm wind go

When day disappears in a glorious show,
Tell me again-where does the twilight go

When storm clouds gather to and fro,
Tell me again-where does the sunshine go

When I am so old, so tired and slow,
Please tell me again-why you love me so.

Prologue to If You Should Go

Have you ever wondered what your
last words to your loved one might be?
Ever wonder what they might say to you?
What would you want to hear?
What would you want to say?

If You Should Go

If you should go and I should stay,
What is it you would have me say.
That I will be near or on my way
Not far behind, not far away?

If I should go and you should stay,
What is it I would have you say.
I'll be there in the blink of an eye-
Cross my heart and hope to die.

Prologue to The Memory Jar

Each and everyone of us has a need to
escape our place from time to time.
The trick is to do it unnoticed.
I find it an enjoyable experience to
watch others as they travel thru
Time and space.

The Memory Jar

That place you go, you know the one-
That place you go to be alone.

I've seen you there from time to time,
Nursing your memories as you play the mime.

I view this drama from afar, as you place
Your memories into your memory jar.

You spin and jump and turn about
As you put them in and take them out.

What a price to the piper you must pay
So you may dance on his gossamer stage.

Then you return to me with a mysterious smile
Never knowing I knew you were gone for awhile.

Prologue to Death

During the early months of 1996 I
was suddenly placed under the knife and
underwent open heart surgery. I
had a total of five bypasses and I
survived with little difficulty.
As time passed I began to realize how
delicate life really is and how fortunate I
had been in my recovery. This
Realization led me to write "DEATH"

Death

Death knocked on my door today
And I think he was here yesterday.
I'll ignore his passion for the dieing game
And linger awhile if it's all the same.

He will be back, he will return
To look me up and to lay me down.
I shall not make it an easy task,
Maybe I'll wear a different mask.

But alas when I die and you say I will,
I'll play the game and ring that bell.
Eternity awaits just a second away,
Perhaps I should be ready anyway.

Prologue to The Wicked Witch

This poem is dedicated to all the fine people who are involved in the research and development of a cure for Alzheimer's disease.

The Wicked Witch

The wicked witch stopped in today,
Stealing in the same old way.
Silently, slowly with a steady pace,
Stealing the magic from behind a face.

Taking more than she leaves behind,
Ever watchful for a gentle mind.
A crafty witch who will steal your soul
And linger awhile to catch the show.

Drifting eyes search the way
For paths forgotten and bygone days.
The past a mystery, long since gone,
A wondering look, a wandering song.

The witch plays a game called fade-away,
She steals your soul and lets you stay
To run the course and bear her sin.
She returns tomorrow to play again.

Prologue to He never danced

We all have known folks who appear to have just missed the bus. Did they not run hard enough or was the bus just to fast for them? They live their lives inside a fringe, never sticking their toe into the pond because of the snapping turtle that may lurk there. They never quite succeed due to a lack of not caring or not trying. They never know the difference. They never triumph over the mundane. So sorry for their loss.

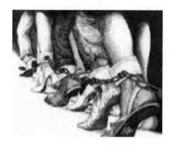

He Never Danced

He never danced, nor did he sing
He never listened to the wind.
Neither did he search for love,
Never lost or found a friend.

He never searched for higher ground,
Never did he stand and fight.
He never shot the rapids straight,
Never praised the starlit night.

Now he is bound for eternity
With no redeeming grace.
No one to see him on his way,
Not a soul who knows his face.

Who can know and who can say
If we have a second chance.
Perhaps in time, and time will tell
If he makes it to another dance.

Prologue to We Are Falling

Recently several of my friends missed roll call. Three of them in thirty days passed on to solve the great mystery. However sobering this is we cannot run and we cannot hide. We all answer one roll call or another on this trip, on this eternal journey.

We Are Falling

We are falling one by one
slowly, quietly it has begun,
one a lover, one a friend
another soul not seen again.

We listen quietly for the sounds
Someone else has made the rounds.
We turn our head and look away,
hopeing only for another day

We are falling one by one
As sunset nears, another's gone,
Seems like just days ago
time was free, time was slow.

Now we are falling one by one
Fading as the setting sun.
Last hurrahs are nearly done
Quietly we are falling one by one.

Tommy Peacock and the Monkey

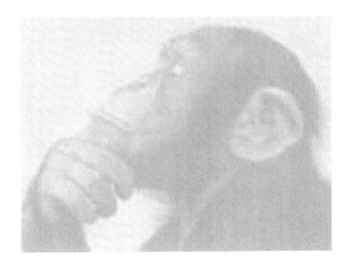

A short story by Wayne Gore

Tommy Peacock and the Monkey

   As a small child I often daydreamed of owning my very own monkey. I often fantasized about the adventures we would have in and around the hills of home. Growing up in the hills of Virginia would have been perfect for such a partnership. My impression of monkeys was about to change during the summer of 1950, the year I turned 10 years old. Rich Creek was a small town of about 500 folks who were pioneer stock and as solid as the timber that surrounded them on every hillside. One early summer morning a new family established residence in our town and as children do we began to investigate this new family. The family consisted of three people, Mr. Peacock-a full bloodied Seminole Indian from the state of Florida, his wife, a white woman and Tommy Peacock who was their natural son. Tommy was my age and would enter school with me in the fall. My friends and I took Tommy into our circle and he quickly adapted to his new surroundings. Tommy was an excellent banjo player for his age and would spend hours practicing. He was quite a bit shorter than the rest of us and had different features but none of us really noticed. Mr. Peacock had settled in our town for the express reason of opening a furniture store since none existed there. Several had tried but none had succeeded so the game was on. Mr. peacock rented a small storefront on a corner downtown with an apartment upstairs where the family would reside.

   Peacock Furniture opened with much fanfare and was enduring the growing pains of a new business with good days and bad days. Mr. Peacock being the entrepreneur he was had a stroke of genius. This was the era that saw Television come of age and Mr. Peacock envisioned everyone in town owning one of these new inventions. Early one morning Mr. Peacock drove out of town in a rented truck on his way to Television land(somewhere in Eastern Virginia) where he purchased a small truckload of table models for sale in his store. The story gets more interesting when another entrepreneur sold

Mr. Peacock a monkey for display purposes in his store. The theory was if the monkey was prominently placed at the store he would draw a lot of attention to the store itself. So with much fanfare the television sets and the monkey arrived home. The monkey was chained to a large cage in front of the store for public viewing. The logic behind this was simple, the good folks would bring their children to see the monkey and while they were there they would buy a new television or some other piece of furniture. What a brilliant idea but no one knew bad fortune was approaching the furniture store faster than a Japanese Bullet train. On many occasions Tommy would tie the monkey to the basket on his bicycle and ride him throughout town showing him off as he went. The monkey was very good natured and was named "Billy" by one of the locals. The name stuck for awhile but would be changed at a later date for obvious reasons.

  At the far end of the block was a tavern where the local drinking club held their regular meetings where they solved all of the town and the worlds problem. These meetings usually occurred Friday night and most of Saturday afternoon. They were fairly mild most of the time. During one of the Saturday meetings the boys decided to walk down the block and check out the monkey that everyone was so excited about. They even took some peanuts from the bar as a welcoming gesture to Billy.
After throwing a few peanuts to the monkey someone switched off to a lit cigarette causing pain to the monkey as he caught it. Then they would revert to peanuts finally confusing the monkey until they switched back to lit cigarettes again. The real topper to this was the beer they slipped to Billy during this process. It can be very hot in Virginia in the summer months so I believe the beer just had to hit the spot with Billy. He mellowed out a little under the influence of the beer but as soon as the hangover kicked in it was open season on the world. These visits occurred for a few weeks but the damage was done. Mr. Peacock finally realized what was

happening and stopped the activities of the drinking club, by then the monkey was violent and had a very aggressive manner. He would attack anyone or anything he could reach, the alternative was to sling anything at you he could get his hands on including his own feces. It does not take a genius to guess what this did for business. Billy stayed outside the store because he could not be trusted in the family apt. or in the store. He would have wreaked havoc to either place. You could say business dropped off as women and children would now cross the street to avoid the store with the mad monkey. During this evolution Billy was renamed "Satan" and it was proving to be appropriate.

One foggy Sept. morn. As we walked to school we noticed Tommy was not waiting for us and we also noticed Billy was not in his cage. As we got closer we noticed the furniture store was desolate and deserted. It seems the Peacock family had left town during the night and it appeared Billy was with them until he was spotted in the other end of town. What sweet revenge it must have been to leave town and leave the mad monkey in the hands of the very ones who had driven him into a full psychosis. We noticed all loose dogs had left town and all of the cats had climbed something high or were hiding under something. Billy wreaked havoc for awhile and silently disappeared from sight. I never saw him again but as an adult I was driving thru town one day after many years away and I thought I saw a brown furry creature in a tree on the edge of town.
The legend of the monkey lives on.

Bobby Hale and the Cowboy Suit

A Short story by Wayne Gore

Bobby Hale and the Cowboy suit

Living in a small town hidden from the world will stir your imagination. You will travel to many places otherwise unattainable and unheard of. Such was the case for me and my outlaw friend Bobby Hale. I was eleven years old and Bobby was about thirteen when fate and bad choices appeared in our lives. The only notable thing about our town was the movie theatre located downtown. The town was small with a grocery store, a drug store and a couple of restaurants, we did have a post office and a small clothing store and the newly defunct Peacock Furniture store. Most every Saturday would find Bobby and myself deeply engrossed in the Saturday afternoon westerns playing at the movie house. Westerns were the fare of the day on Saturdays starting at one pm and running until about ten o'clock at night. We often staggered to the street bleary eyed after seeing a double feature two times. We chased the cattle rustlers and bank robbers all over the wild west with Tom Mix and Hopalong Cassidy. We lived the parts and were convinced we had cowboy blood in our veins.

Bobby lived about a hundred yards from me and we would pick each other up on the way to town for our forays into misadventure. Bobby was older than I was and much more accomplished in the ways of the world. He was an excellent piano player and really knew a lot about girls which impressed me. He was training me for the gallows and I was an excellent student. On this particular Saturday we were exploring the newly opened clothing store and we discovered the Holy Grail of all teenage cowboys. There in all of its glorious splendor was an original, one of a kind, amazing cowboy suit. It took our breath away, we were not prepared for the adrenalin rush we felt just seeing this wonderful display only a few feet away. It was complete with woolen chaps, (later discovered to be cotton), with a large hat . The shirt, pants, gun and holster were all specially made for Tom Mix of this we were sure. After careful examination and deep thinking we both secretly and unanimously came to the same conclusion. The Cowboy suit would be ours. We plotted our scheme with much daring never giving thought to the aftermath, never considering how we would explain to parents or other kids or store owners how we were able to possess such a prize.

  The plan was simple, I was to distract the store owner and Bobby would simply steal the suit and we would trade off wearing it. It worked out it was a pretty good plan since bobby stuffed the entire Suit under his lightweight jacket and was gone in a flash. Once outside it was no less exciting than a successful bank robbery. Bobby being the leader was naturally entitled to wear the suit first so we headed home so he could make the change from average small boy to superhero. I could never envision what bobby's father must have thought when he first saw the transformation that took place in his living room. Looking back over the years I have decided all small boys have a stupid gene that kicks in during the early years, This was about the time ours stepped up to the plate. Mr. Hale for some unknown reason wanted to know where in H__ Bobby had got the suit and Bobby immediately told him I had purchased it and it was too large for me so I had given it to Bobby. Can you imagine Bobby's disbelief when his father decided to come to my house and further investigate this matter.

  I was standing in the dirt road in front of my house and my grandfather was sitting on the porch when I spied Mr. Hale coming up the road with Bobby lagging behind with the suit tucked under his arm. I sensed a fear I have never felt again to this very day. I knew in a few short minutes my life would be over but I nevertheless swore an oath to never again participate in any crime as long as I lived. Bobby stuttered and I stammered as this crime was unfolded and laid on our shoulders. We both were made to return the suit with sincere apologies and we were never to interact with each other again and we were grounded for twenty-five years . Childhood whippings were not uncommon in Virginia in the early fifties so I will leave the punishment at that. As Bobby started home I watched my grandfather stand in the road and throw rocks at him as he scurried home. I lost contact with Bobby over the years and it was not until thirty five years later we would finally talk about the Cowboy suit since the twenty-five year grounding rule had elapsed.

Barneys Wooden Leg

A short story by Wayne Gore

Barney's Wooden Leg

   Much of the following events I know to be true because I personally observed them. The rest of the events have been filled in by friends and common sense. I was about twelve years old when these events started unfolding. I lived in a small Virginia town with my dad and his grandparents. My grandfather was retired and my grandmother took in boarders to make ends meet. My father was unemployed most of his life, and was a serious connoisseur of anything distilled or fermented. He did not work because he chose not to, and he drank for the same reason, he chose too. Occasionally he would take on a small handyman job somewhere in town so he could raise the capital for one of his tea parties as he called them. Tea Parties were drinking binges lasting several days and were held on a small sandy spot by the banks of the New River. Attending would be my father and several of his associates. We lived in a large three story house halfway up the hill as you leave town. It had been a railroad boarding house at one time and was well suited for grandmas boarders. The town was small with little fluctuation in the population, there was a gas station, a drug store, and a post office and restaurant. A grocery store ,a bank and an adjoining barber shop. Of course as with most river bottom towns it had a railroad running adjacent to the main route through town. The town of Olive Branch was built along the banks of the New River and was surrounded on the other sides by a mountain range. It was a peaceful town supported by a manufacturing plant some ten or twelve miles away. There were a few small farmers and merchants to round out the mix. Most days you would find my grandfather and my father sitting on the front porch watching traffic come and go on the hillside as they rolled their cigarettes from a Prince

Albert can. Days came and went in an uneventful flow except for the occasional tea party my father would conduct. These events were controlled by cash or lack of cash. There were several locals who would participate in this event but none as loyal as Barney. He was a willing participant on all occasions. Barney Jackson was an unmarried man living in town with his mother. He worked at the manufacturing plant as some sort of craftsman and worked on the side as a sign painter and was a very talented painter. Barney would supplement his income painting signs on the windows of the local businesses. On Saturdays you could often see Barney roaming from shop to shop looking for a sign painting assignment. Barney was small in stature and large in personality weighing about 150 lbs. at 5 ft. 6 inches tall. He always had a funny story to tell and would amuse you at any opportunity. There were a couple more local rounders who would show up for the party but they lacked the dedication and stamina necessary to run the full course. They would eventually drop out and head for home. The tea parties were held on the beach and would run for several days ending when the wine or cash supply was diminished. The participants simply stayed there and drank themselves into oblivion lying on an old blanket or cardboard and stoking a wood fire. Their place at the beach was between the river and the railroad tracks about 200 feet away. away. Steam locomotives would run daily, once in each direction. The tea party members would loudly discuss all of the local problems and then the world problems would be discussed. It was a bond I had never seen before and have not seen since. I remember checking on the two of them from time to time realizing they were relatively safe. No one from town would bother them. The biggest enemies they had at this juncture were the Baptists who roamed the streets of town like guard dogs. They would eventually return to life with hangovers so severe I can only imagine their intensity. After the heat from the families died down it was back to the porch for my father and back to work for Barney until the next Tea Party.

  Barney fell into a trap a lot of men fall into, he fell in love with an unattainable woman. The woman in question worked in the same plant as Barney only in an adjoining department. The two relevant features of Nadine was the fact she was unmarried and she had only one leg. Nadine had been involved in a car crash some years before and lost her left leg just below the knee. She was a pretty and outgoing woman who had never married because she believed anyone who would marry her would do so only out of pity and she relayed this concept to Barney. Nevertheless Barney turned on his charm and impacted Nadine emotionally, convincing her he was ready her if she would only have him. Nadine and Barney maintained a relationship for some months and Barney was wearing Nadine down. This played with Barney's emotions and reasoning and finally Barney reached the conclusion that Nadine was trying to tell him something at a subliminal level. No one can say Barney acted in anything close to a rational manner. During the course of several months and a couple of Tea Parties Barney made a decision unlike any rational human would make unless they were in love. Near the end of the rainy season somewhere in May Barney and dad held a Tea Party that lasted the better part of the weekend. My father was always the last one to leave the beach when they had been partying but for some unforeseen reason he left first this time. This left Barney, who was in a fragile mental state alone at the beach. What happened next will never be understood by any mortal I have ever met. Whether it was an accident or done deliberately we will never know. That secret lies buried with Barney.

On his way home in an intoxicated state Barney had to cross the railroad tracks to get to the road. Some say Barney lay his leg across the track and the steam locomotive took off his leg just below the knee.
Others say it was providence at work and just an unfortunate accident. Whatever happened Barney was now a one legged man just like his Nadine. Months of healing both emotionally and physically followed Barney but he was up to the challenge. He was convinced once he was ambulatory he would have no problem obtaining the love of his life, Nadine. Now no one could say Barney was feeling sorry for Nadine now that they both had a missing appendage. Barney started out with crutches and after several long months he was fitted with a new so called wooden leg. Of course it was not wooden but some new age plastic that had only recently been developed. Barney handled the crutches with ease and after much practice he became very proficient with his new leg. Soon he was back to work and even attended a tea party. He could be seen about town walking around with only a slight hitch in his step. I can only imagine the meeting that took place between Barney and Nadine when he returned to work. Barney was now ready to pursue Nadine with a full head of steam.
I was told in private and in confidence that Barney was unsure of Nadine's reaction to these events and he blurted out to her that he wanted to marry her and for her to please consider the sacrifice he had made for her. This was taken to mean he had deliberately placed his leg on the track for the train to amputate his leg. There must have been a stunned silence and a cloud of disbelief when Nadine replied to Barney she could never marry a man who would do such a foolish thing. Barneys world ceased to spin for a few months as he made another adjustment. Nadine quit her job and moved back home to another part of the state. The Tea Parties continued with more fervor than ever as the problems of the world were

put in their proper place. The last Tea Party I recall
was out of the ordinary, to say the least. The party was in full swing when Barney took his wooden leg off to increase his comfort and shortly thereafter he went to sleep or just passed out. With Barney we could never be sure. A few days prior to this party there had been heavy rain upstream and in the name of flood control the dam had unleashed some extra water,
This high water hit the beach about the time Barney was out of it and he awoke just in time to see his leg floating downstream. The leg was never seen again
and I don't know how Barney got home or how he explained it but he was on crutches for a long time afterwards. I don't wonder so much about Barney but I do from time to time wonder about the destiny of the wooden leg. Imagine if you will the leg continuing on to the next big river and the one after that and eventually reaching the ocean. Suppose after a few years it was to wash up on some south sea island that had never seen a white man. What would the natives take this omen to be. Would they place it on some makeshift altar and worship it or would they curse it as the devil?.

Grandmas Crock-pot

A short Story by Wayne Gore

Grandmas Crockpot

During the early days of railroads and coalmining in Southwest Virginia railroad boarding houses were Established, owned and operated by the railroads. At the end of a long run the workmen would need a place to spend the night before their long trip back home. This was the most economical and practical way to curb expenses and rooms could be let to other travelers if they were available. These boarding houses were there for the convenience of the railroads but they also accommodated other travelers who might need an overnight resting place. I grew up in such a boarding house although it was no longer owned or operated by the railroad. It was a three story with a tin roof sitting on the side of a hill In the small town of Rich Creek Virginia. Air conditioners were unheard of in those day. You could touch the tin roof from inside the attic on a hot summer day and it would blister your hand. The house was purchased by my grandparents and operated by my grandmother.

  My grandmother was a staunch God fearing women who quoted scripture daily. It seems she was was driven by a burning desire to save me from perdition. I led two lives as a youngster; one life was in pursuit of living up to grandma's view of what a teenager should be, and the other life was in search of golden idols and dastardly deeds. Pretty much the same things all teenage boys chase, There were six members of the family and after you add a dozen boarders you get a pretty good picture of who ate last. Most of the time that was me since I was the youngest. I developed a reach that far exceeded my years. Boarders, as they were called, would be construction workers, road workers and high line construction workers. I lived with my grandparents from first grade on and was blessed with a lot of freedom to roam and do as I wished. I fished and roamed the hills and hunted wild game, always looking for something new and exciting to do.

We had a garden in back where we grew most of our vegetables, and had a chicken house on the side of the hill with about thirty chickens. It was my job to feed the chickens and hoe the garden, as needed. Down from the garden near the kitchen window was a beautiful grape arbor adorned with large blue Concord grapes. I loved these grapes and waited faithfully until they ripened each year. These very same grapes would nearly be my downfall with my grandmother but her forgiving nature would show through and I would be spared from the penitentiary and or a horrible existence as a wino. Red Fred and I decided we (meaning me) would make some homemade wine since we had all of the necessary ingredients at hand. Now Red Fred, my closest and dearest friend, had a gene somewhere in his being that occasionally erupted and led him into temporary madness. This is the same gene all teenage boys have and it is a constant struggle to combat it. It leads teenage boys to do strange and stupid things like making homemade wine in the attic of the house in your grandma's crock pot. We did our research and stocked up on the necessary ingredients for this venture. The research consisted of asking other teenage boys our own age who had not a clue, but plenty of advice and opinions. After a few days of thought and discussion the game was on. Since there were no stairs or electricity in the third floor attic, I had to lift myself and the necessary products up manually. This was perfect since grandma could not get into the attic without the use of a stepladder.

After making several trips to the attic with grocery sacks full of grapes I began the squashing process and adding what we thought would be the proper amounts of sugar and yeast(borrowed from grandma along with her five gallon crock pot). At this point I covered the crock pot with a loose knit fabric to let it breath and to keep the bugs out. On later reflection the addition of a few bugs might have enhanced the flavor of the concoction. We, meaning our teenage brain trust had decided about fourteen days of the heated attic should render our required results so we began the long agonizing wait. I had the home field advantage since I lived just under the attic. This meant I could sneak a peek and a taste whenever I chose. I would grab a flashlight and pull myself into the attic daily to make my check. As the days drug on grandma announced she could not find her crock pot and that puzzled her since she had a place for everything. She also stated the grapes just outside the kitchen window were putting out a rather strong aroma you could smell all over the house. She found this to be strange and commented on it several times as she searched for her crock pot. It was dark in the attic since it was not wired for electricity and with the flashlight on it seemed as if I were in the middle of a blue fog.

The next step in this adventure was the bottling process. So Red Fred and I collected about two dozen R.C. Cola bottles and corks and the filling and smuggling began. Into the attic I went and began to fill bottles and cork them. Nowhere had we read about straining this product so it never happened. I did, however, pick the largest stems and debris out of the crock pot therefore completing the procedure. The aroma throughout the house had reached the stench stage along with grandmas patience over the disappearance of her crock pot. The time had come to bring this venture to a conclusion so I began the removal of the bottled wine from the attic. This was accomplished by me stuffing a bottle into my waist band so I could have both hands free to swing myself down from the attic. I made several successful trips to a remote location where Red Fred and myself stashed our treasure for future

use. As fate always does, it decided to rear its ugly head as I was making a trip out of the attic the same time grandma happened to climb the stairs. As I swung down and landed on the floor the downward force caused the bottle to release from my waistband and slide down my pants leg exploding as it hit the floor.
Everything after that is a big blue haze and that is how grandma described the event as she finally returned to sanity. My life would never be the same again for a long time. I remember the aroma and blue wine covering the wallpaper and the floor and ceiling. It appeared a blue bomb had exploded in the hallway. I remember scrubbing the floor and the crock-pot for many hours trying to remove the stain. The lesson I learned from this is if you have a craving for wine be sure you buy it in a store.

The Watermelon Truck

A short story by Wayne Gore

The Watermelon Truck

Has there ever been a young man who did not crave adventure and danger as he battled acne and adolescence? I speak of the male gender because I have been there. When you understand the forces that drive teenage boys to stretch their wings and push their boundaries then you will have gained valuable insight Into their forays into dark regions not explored by sane and simple people. I turned fourteen years old during the summer of 1953 and I was judged as mentally inadequate by more than one person in our small town.

I was tall and thin for my age, standing five feet seven and weighing in at 135 pounds. I was a good runner with excellent endurance developed by walking and running the mountains and hills of Virginia where I grew up. Our town of Rich Creek was placed there by God and was bounded by a mountain range and a river. It was a small town by any standard. It had one gas stations, a post office, drug store, grocery store and a small grade school. About 400 people called Rich Creek home and it was a quiet safe place to be. Often driven by boredom and an insanity clause that was included with our birth certificates we teenage boys would slip out of our confined lives and attempt some dastardly deed. There were four of us in the main posse and a few fringe members who were talkers and not doers, the kind that had to be in by dark and who brushed their teeth before bed. This was not the case with the Four Horsemen as we called ourselves.

Included was Red, tall like myself with long legs and a head of hair that had been set on fire by the devil. His Christian name was Fred and he had freckles as large as nickels all over his body. Fred was up for anything and was experimenting with chewing tobacco and sleeping late, although not at the same time. Fred was just always around. Next in line was shorty, his given name was Ronald Flowers and he lived up to his nickname. He was only five feet tall and built like a stump, strong and eager for adventure. Shorty was starting to notice girls and had a burning desire to see how many waffles he could eat. He often told us he believed he could be the waffle eating champion of the world if given the opportunity. Next came Mike who we dubbed mikey. Mikey was laid back and offered a quiet presence and not much more other than following us about and offering his services in our nefarious schemes. Mikey wore bib overalls and a baseball hat and was strong for his age and size, a good looking kid who would later on in life become a Baptist Minister.

The greatest advantage of growing up in a small southern town is mastering your imagination. During the summer months of school recess we were left to our own devices . Since there was very little television and no electrical devices to occupy us we had to invent our own means of entertainment. We would ride cows(not horses) and we would dynamite fish in the creek beds. We called it dynamiting but we had no access to dynamite so we would use carbide. Carbide was a white powdery substance used in coal miners lamps to provide light when in the mines. It was flammable and if used correctly you could contain it in a mason jar, sink it in a creek bed and wait for a small explosion. This would stun the fish then all you had to do was pick them up. Illegal but awesome. Money was hard to come by so we were forever on the lookout for ways and means to increase our finances. I remember Red Fred (that's what we called Fred) lurking behind the local grocery store and lifting as many empty pop bottles as he could load into a paper bag and then enter the front of the store and sell them back to the owner for two cents apiece. This eventually stopped when the owner finally figured out his inventory of bottles was not increasing.

Occasionally there would be an opportunity to mow someone's lawn but there were no gas powered mowers in those days, push mowers were the standard of the day. Most summer days we would swim in the river that bounded the town on one side, the town was in a valley about a mile long. State route 460 ran off one side of the valley thru town and at the other end of town it started upward back onto a mountain range. As you came into town from the hillside the speed limit would immediately drop to twenty miles per hour through town and as soon as you cleared town you started back up the other hill.

Needless to say if you were driving a truck through town it would be frustrating since you could not get a full run at the uphill climb out of town. During these early days trucks were not the fine polished machines they are today. They were mostly manufactured to late forties standards, heavy, cumbersome and completely lacking in driver amenities such as radios and air conditioners. We would often stand on the bridge at the end of town and watch for out of state traffic and large trucks to pass. Wondering where they were going and where they had been. Route 460 was a heavily traveled road since the interstate system was only a rumor to this part of the world.

As we were standing on the bridge one fine day we noticed a lowboy flatbed truck full of watermelons heading north. It came through town at the customary low speed and started up the hill out of town at a low crawl. The watermelons were piled in back of the trailer with no covering on them. We had noticed these trucks in the past and surmised they were coming from Georgia or South Carolina on their way to market somewhere up north. There was no doubt it was a watermelon truck. It was at this instant Red Fred commented on how easy it would be to just pick one off a slow moving truck. That was all it took, the great Rich Creek watermelon caper was in the works. Planning began immediately and soon we were waiting for just the right moment and the right truck to appear. Nothing more appeared that day much to our disappointment so next afternoon we stationed ourselves in what we thought to be strategic positions. We had reasoned that two of us would climb onto the rear of the truck and simply hand watermelons down to two of us on the ground as we trotted along. Red Fred and myself were to stay on the ground since we were taller and had a longer reach. Mikey and Shorty would climb onto the rear of the truck and hand the melons down and we would lay them on the ground and go for another one. We calculated we could easily liberate a dozen melons without much danger. We believed the driver would not be able to stop the truck pulling such a grade or he would never get started again. Since there was no place to pull off all we had to worry about was cars following behind the truck and we were watching for them. We waited patiently and it was about to pay off, coming through town was a watermelon truck loaded to the top. We began to execute our plan, it worked without any difficulty, up went Mikey and Shorty and the melons started coming. I missed one and it hit the ground with a thud exploding and covering me with a red mist. The driver saw what was happening and with disbelief began shouting obscenities at us at the top of his voice. The truck was so loud we could not hear him but we got the message. It worked like a Swiss watch and we were in and out so to speak in just a few minutes. Slowly the truck disappeared into the mountain range and was gone forever. We had thirteen melons to do with as we pleased. Since we were not very far from the creek we moved the melons to the creek and submerged them in cool creek water. We then ate more melon than we thought was possible. The next day when the melons were cool from the creek water we began selling them door to door for fifty cents apiece. We ended up with a couple bucks apiece which was a lot on money for us.

We explained to our customers that the melons were homegrown and part of an FFA project so everyone was happy. Occasionally one of the town ladies would ask us when we would have some more melons. We considered expanding our operation to the Cantaloupe market but never followed through on it. This is not the only time we did this, but we lost our nerve when one of the trucks found a turnaround spot on top of the hill and came back into town looking for us. The driver of the truck was afraid to park his truck in town due to obvious reasons. Luckily he never found us but the word was out. The next year the new Turnpike opened and the watermelon trucks disappeared from Route 460 forever. I still love watermelon to this day.

The Minstrel Show

THE MINSTREL SHOW

    Looking back at my life in the western part of Virginia during the 40's and the 50's is similar, I think, to observing life in another land. What was true then no longer applies today and the truths we recognize today would have been intolerable to many that existed in that far away place so long ago. I wonder about those things we trust today, Will they be trustworthy for our children and grandchildren or will they become relics and just fade away. Will we betray our children and grandchildren with our own adopted and deceptive truths.

    During my teenage years in this southern cocoon I lived in a world of absolutes and unknowns. Some things were absolutely true, and everything else existed in a gray area or just did not matter. There was an unknown place where all of the unknowns existed and we did not trouble ourselves with these matters. I lived in a small town of about four hundred people who could be described as good folk. The town was on the banks of a large river and was very similar to most of the towns on the river. The population of this valley was supported by a textile mill some six miles away. There were also a few farmers and merchants to round out the valley. The people of this hamlet had the same concerns about their future that other Americans had. It seemed everyone knew or had a relative in a faraway place

called Korea. Typically the general topic of conversation was the local football team and their prospects, The world series was listened to on the radio since television would not appear until
 We were convinced the government would not lie to us, Promises were made, and promises were kept and it was a way of life. We would remain naive until the Viet Nam war relieved us of our innocence. Church on Sunday was a way of life, and discipline was maintained in the classrooms. Everyone knew everyone else and electronic communication was through party line. It was a sleepy mountain town, hot in the summer and very cold in the winter.

 One of the exceptions that existed was the absence of any Black or Hispanic people in our geographic area. They simply did not exist in our local culture with the exception of a few families that dwelled some nine miles from us. They had their own school and most of them worked in the nearest hospital or local restaurants. They were very seldom seen or heard and they were just who they were. They were never discussed or disparaged that I can recall. We were not taught to fear them or to hate them ,we were taught nothing about them other than what we learned in social studies in school.

 Our town had its own identity and was known for certain things, among them was the Annual Minstrel Show held in the late fall of each year. Minstrel Shows were popular in the South and had been since the Civil War. It was a show sponsored by whites and all roles were done by whites. Everyone was in blackface playing southern blacks as ignorant, poor and a superstitious lot generally happy in their social setting. It was a two hour show with an intermission and was held at the local movie theater on a Thursday, Friday and Saturday night. The setting was an Interlocutor (master of ceremonies) and a large painted canvas as a backdrop. The interlocutor was the only white face on the stage and he was well dressed and obviously of a higher social standing than anyone else on the stage. The backdrop canvas was painted as an old southern plantation with large bales of cotton on each end of the stage for the end men as they were called. Jokes flew and Banjos were played and there was singing and dancing to no end. The end men were outrageous characters who told jokes and generally pandered to the Interlocutor as they bantered with each other about their current misdemeanors and situations. This endeavor was sponsored by a national fraternal organization that exists today and is easily recognizable for its charitable works. The purpose of the show was to raise funds for various charities; therefore, it was considered a noble pursuit. This event was a yearly event and long anticipated by everyone throughout the county. All players were local and everyone from seven to seventy could participate as long as they had a talent or the nerve to try out. I was successful three years running during my early teens. I auditioned and was accepted as part of the chorus along with another six or seven members. I was caught up in the excitement of it all as were my friends as we sang in blackface. Rehearsals lasted about six weeks and were very private, Nothing was leaked to the public as the anticipation mounted. The script was purchased for an outside source and was very expensive. The big draw from my peer group and myself was the party that was to be held at the end of the run, Parties were a rare thing for us and we eagerly awaited the event.

A good time was had by all at the show and no one gave a thought to the political correctness or the subliminal nature of our endeavor. It was simply a part of our culture and any suggestion of racial undertones would have been dismissed as trivial. I have since wondered how I would have felt had I been a Black man and had seen this show with its display of oblique racism. This type of racism was knee deep in our society and we did not even know it was there.
Throughout my short tenure with the Minstrel show I never had any idea it was racist or derogatory and that was a shortcoming of my own. For that I am truly sorry.

Made in the USA
Columbia, SC
02 July 2022